TOTAL ECLIPSE

Poems by Waco Porter

Kansas City Spartan Press Missouri

Spartan Press
Kansas City, Missouri
spartanpresskc.com

Copyright (c) Waco Porter 2017
First Edition 1 3 5 7 9 10 8 6 4 2
ISBN: 978-1-946642-00-4
LCC#: 2017930802

Design, edits and layout: Jason Ryberg, J.D. Tulloch
Author photo: Sharon Eiker
Cover photo: Jon Bidwell
All rights reserved. No part of this publication may be reproduced or transmitted in any form or by any means, electronic or mechanical, including photocopying, recording or by info retrieval system, without prior written permission from the author.

ACKNOWLEDGMENTS

Prospero's Books and Spartan Press would like to thank
Jeanette Powers, J. D. Tulloch, Jason Preu, M. Scott
Douglass, Shawn Pavey, Shaun Savings, Jesse Kates,
Jim Holroyd, Steven H.Bridgens, Thomas Mason,
Beth Dille, Mason Wolf, Katherine Samet, The West Plaza
Tomato Co., Mark Mclane, the Osage Arts Community
and The Robert J. Deuser Foundation For Libertarian
Studies.

The author would like to thank Jump Start Arts,
Spartan Press, Sharon Eiker, Jeanette Powers
and Jason Ryberg

CONTENTS

Checkout Line / 1

Reaching Out (feeling the void) / 2

Slow Motion / 3

Porter Girls / 4

Tendencies / 6

Drinking Alone / 7

Full Eclipse / 8

Final Sprint / 9

Letters That Don't Get Mailed / 10

Heartbreaker — Simone / 11

Swap Meet / 11

Armee / 11

Waterfalls / 12

Trigger Finger / 12

Security Risk / 12

Message To A Friend / 13

Coy I Tuss / 13

Los Manos / 13

Watchman / 14

Not A Mouse / 14

At The Gate / 14

New Additions / 15

Nostalgia / 16

Chimera / 17

Pick-A-Nick Basket / 18

Champ / 19

Details / 20

Saggy Boobs And Baby Fat —
  Mother Talking To Son / 21
Windy Day Walking / 22
My Daughter As A Woman / 23
Make Believe Vs. Imagination / 24
39th Street / 25
Cast Away / 26
Evolove / 27
The Divide / 28
Baby Talk / 29
Broken Glass / 31
two / sixteen / twenty eleven / 32
S.I.P. / 33
Rustic Vision — Black Kids / 34
Passions Of Women / 35
Fat Bellies And Fireflies — Sydnee / 36
Animal Planit / 37
Wake Up Calls / 38
February 15 — / 39
Lick-O-Wish / 40
Strike A Pose / 41
Diary Entries / 42
Apostle Letter / 43
Baby Doll — / 44
bRainstorm / 45
Good Medicine / 46
Dagum / 47

Inns And Outs / 48

Finish Line / 49

I Suppose, I 'Spose / 50

The Ritual / 51

Daddy's Girls / 52

August / 53

Vermont To Woodson / 54

Kritchuh / 55

Passion Of Men / 56

For Waco, Liz, Nell, Alice, Marie, Sheila, Sydnee, Simone, and Vanessa. Thank you for keeping me supplied with beautiful memories.

Checkout Line

You're beautiful
And I'm lonely,
How much to get rid of this feeling,
How much for the healing,
How much for the medicine,
The remedy that cures the state I'm in,
How much for you to spread beautiful all over me
Tend to my extremities
Leave and let me sleep peacefully,
How much to reverse the flow of poison away
From my heart
To send blood to the other parts,
How much to touch nether regions
And breathe out while I ease in,
How much that you might spelunk or smother stuff,
How much for you to squeak and squeal
And wear these heals,
How much for a friend or two,
Whatever gets you to something new,
How much for backseats and city parks,
Alley ways or anywhere dark,
How much for public indecency
Public anything,
How much for shame and embarrassment
When the game turns into harassment.

I'm sorry
Yes,
I'll take plastic,
And no bag for the milk.

Reaching Out (feeling the void)

Single male, 6'1", brown eyes, black hair, muscular build, non-smoker. Enjoys great food and good conversation. Values healthy relationships built on trust, commitment, and friendship. If you feel the same and want to meet someone who is looking for unconditional love, I would like to hear from you and possibly share some quality time.

Slow Motion

if
its
slow
in
time
there
is
a
possibility
that
it
might
be
perfect
butifitsfastitwontlastaslong

Porter Girls

Daddies don't cry for baby girls —
>Not when he knows time heals all wounds
>Even if he sickens with worry and doubt,

Daddies don't cry for baby girls —
>He turns all the lights off and checks the locks,
>He daydreams about the first day of school,
>And has nightmares about first loves heartbreak,
>He works longer hours
>so he can put extra change in change jars,
>Bank accounts and piggy banks

Daddies don't cry for baby girls —
>He pays for prom dresses and weddings,
>and pretends to like fiancés and boyfriends,
>He remembers running beside her on her first
>bike, showing her off at work,
>and hunting for the right outfit,
>He remembers her smile,
>and does everything he can to see it every day,
>even if it's just before she falls asleep,

Daddies don't cry for baby girls —
>He embarrasses her in front of her friends
>by just being there,
>And becomes her hero by being there,
>He lives for the moment he is a witness
>to her being the envy of her friends
>and pats himself on the back,

>He hates to say he can't afford it,
>I'm not going to make it, or I forgot

Daddies don't cry for baby girls —
>He cries at graduation, the wedding, letting go,
>and kisses good bye

Daddies don't cry for baby girls —
>He picks her up again for the first time
>kisses her mother
>and takes them home.

Tendencies

I'm dead beyond the realm of God and reason,
In fact, I've died so many times
That my breath as it appears in cold air
    is my true physical form,
Everything I've learned up to now
    has brought me no joy, happiness, or satisfaction,
Even though I'm here as living proof,
I am a mere stepping stone
    in the succession of events of someone else's life,
I'm here,
As proof that I exist,
Yet I am a mere stepping stone in the
    succession of events of someone else's existence,
Their life,
Mine is happenstance,
Events so few and far between,
My legs were not designed for this game of leap frog.
My life as it were is how I shall regard it
    from here on in,
Wherever it may go.
Suicide notes for a letter I will never write.

Drinking Alone

There's silence in my mind-
A vibrancy I can't find anywhere
Except here
Amongst God's creations
And I want them hushed —
Shushed so the imagery is not tainted
Painted with poor technique —
Long careful strokes and no abstractions
This was meant to be a portrait
Not an interdimensional undertaking
There'll be no splashing of color,
Or mixing of media,
No sly grins or obscure placement of the nose
No overuse of color to give a glimpse of human
Shape and ideas
This is Richard Gallo
Sitting at the end of the couch.
This is the guitar player,
This is a toast to Emily St. Claire,
This is my tea —
With honey, lemon, and two fingers of McCormick's.
My permanent collection.

Full Eclipse

I am employing assistance to sketch perfection,
The troubled man's shaky hand
Demonizes the curves of the frame,
Overlooks the fine detail,
Is entertained by a mid-summer night dream,
Knowing all too well
The full moon pushes currents to shore,
Uncovers madness,
Brings brighter light the crescent moon
Cannot provide.

Final Sprint

Sky's alive amidst divine light
My sights askew from the day
    Brighter than I ever knew.
My best attempt to shuffle quicker
Are met with angst,
And the paining thought
It can't be maintained
My chest is pounding and my heart is crying
Starving for more as I stumble
And allow my brain to send a message to all to
    Enjoy the day
    Take it in
But shattered glass on the path wakes the giant saying
    Fight for the mile
    Stumble if you will
But chase away the crying heart.

Letters That Don't Get Mailed

My Love,

I'm sorry for your life. I'm sorry for the responsibilities you have that you're not ready for; babies and bills that never disappear. I'm sorry you've missed out on better things and what you've settled for will never match your dreams or foolishness. I'm sorry that I'll never leave you. I know I'm not what you hoped for, but you're everything I'm not. I'm sorry you will never read this. I can't take the chance you finding out how I feel. I wish I could let you go on to a different life, maybe a better life even if you wish. But I can't gamble on maybe or maybe not finding someone I admire as much as I do you. You are *it* for me and consequently that means I am *it* for you. In case you're wondering, I am prepared to do what one might deem *inappropriate.* Just please remember I love you and the kids and am willing to do anything to keep it all together or, at least the appearance of such. All my love.

Heartbreaker – Simone

You make me wonder if love is enough
Cause
Everything isn't broken,
But we are in need of repair.

Swap Meet

When forever dies,
You'll miss me when I'm gone

Armee

Open wide, open wide
Above your head, by your side
Draping and wrapping boa like
Constricting fear, anger, and loneliness.

Waterfalls

baby girls get tired and cry
big girls get tired of crying

Trigger Finger

I'm glad fingers don't shoot bullets;
I don't want to see where you're hurting
When I point out your imperfections.

Security Risk

Here's to a good life,
Safe travels and a safe flight,
Hopefully a slight in judgement
Won't lead to blunt trauma

Message To A Friend

I'm in God's hands now
Impaired
Imprisoned
Imbalanced
Impotent
In need

Coy I Tuss

by day we play into nights' delight
by night our delights make way to day's light.

Los Manos

Pull galaxies to your breast
And nourish the universe.

Watchman

The observing eye often lies,
Lives cannot be deconstructed so easily,
It takes more time.

Not A Mouse

Foxes at play
Night and day
Doesn't matter the cat
Be here or away

At The Gate

So what happened?
I thought if I jumped into the crowd
I'd be one of them.

Maybe you should have screamed louder.

New Additions

My babies have added —
Years to my face
Miles to my feet
Tenderness to my hands
Humbleness to my heart

Nostalgia

Every now and then
God awakens my hope for life,
Another day to do well,
Be thankful for space and time,
Friends and acquaintances,
Reasons to laugh and memories you can't control.
Hope for life outside of safety zones,
It may not be home,
But home is so far away.
Where else can you rest your bones
And hum a few notes,
To something you just remembered once was.

Chimera

I love you
Then the rains came
Washed the chimera away
Exposing —
Bald spots
Crows feet
A wandering eye
A furrowing brow
Sour lips
A bitter tongue
Crooked teeth
Slump shoulders
A curving spine
An aging chest
Love handles
Cracked skin
Unhealed wounds
Unexplained bruises
Odd hair growth
Weak hands
Crooked limbs
Stumbling feet
Do you still love me?

Pick-A-Nick Basket

Dine with me on memories,
We'll feast on us exclusively,
Toast to the past explicitly,
Drink to the future intuitively,
Embrace each moment religiously,
Serenade you for a lifetime copiously.

Champ

Wrestle your life young man,
Don't go for the b.s. 3 count you see on television
that gets blanket applause for a good show,
Go for the KO,
Go for the knockout that puts -
> crowd's in silence
> fear in your enemies
> and respect in your corner

Don't leave it to the judges to proclaim the victor,
Get your bearings and put life on its ass,
Then look down at it writhing in pain
and put two hands in the air to collect
high fives from your maker.

Cause had the tables been turned,
Life would stand over you and piss on your misery.

Details

Your life may not be poetry
but,
those insignificant details and monotonous tasks
that get done in blank minded routine,
somehow become lines of thought,
and waking moments of clarity
that do more than you ever imagined.

Saggy Boobs And Baby Fat —
Mother Talking To Son

Can we live out the magical day
When your father comes home?
Your father —
Wide eyed
Restless
Calculating
And persistent to no avail
He charmed me out of my dreams
I fell in love with his
We rode his fantasy
He navigated with ingenuity
Until I was ready to stay back in reality.
Now, here you are chasing that same star —
But I wish your father would return
For 2 seconds
To prepare you to travel beyond my reach.

Windy Day Walking

I wish I could tickle the leaves the way you do
I laugh with them these days — cold as they are,
End of thought

My Daughter As A Woman

Leaving my neck and kisses behind
Fulfilling promises she made to herself
Seeing her mother as woman equal,
Yet
Of a different grain
We don't remember the firsts the same
    She remembers the pain of falling,
    And the wonder of doing it alone,
    I remember the wonder of saving the day,
    And the pain of seeing her do it alone,
But she'll be back soon,
She promised

Make Believe Vs. Imagination

Take a chance that the story exist in reality,
All the possibilities are the realities of anyone,
From beginning to end its own anomaly.

Just enjoy the ride,
Pace at warp speed,
To the other side.

39th Street

The locals aren't moths to flames,
For the bright lights and reward cards for key chains,
We can't be sucked in to the luster

Muster to the home base —
Unrefined, obscure places
For just a taste of what emits from a classic.

Cast Away

Long since gone
>	Opening lines of songs
>	Palm holding Psalms
>	Warding off it all.

Long since gone
>	Far from home
>	A few days travel
>	Movin on.

Long since gone
>	Calm the alarm
>	Don't mean no harm
>	Still they swarmed.

Long since gone
>	Embellished wrongs
>	The throngs were gongs
>	They got what they want.

Evolove

Love is changing still
It is evolving from the former creature it used to be
It is revolving around the center point of relationships
Going through changes as all things natural —
> Experiencing new life,
> Sustaining existence through adversity
> And dying to make way for the cycle to return

It is revolutionizing motivations and conjuring up
New ways to begin the affair,
It is revolting against extinction,
And seeking an environment
That will allow a natural existence to maintain itself
Through changes

The Divide

Sky blue
And I want to dive head first
Kick past the reef
To fantasies of a different hue.
Royal blue
And each stroke reaches, grabs, pulls
And pushes to foot
Dreams of a different hue.
Cobalt blue
Cruising at 25 knots
A true master and commander
Deserving salute from a royal crew
Gales coming from the southwest
To premonitions of a different hue
Steel blue
And not another shadow on the surface
The silver linings provide cover
For the bluest eye
So have I
Truest eyes facing the divide.

Baby Talk

And the babies say yes
Despite the blood, crying, and pushing
Despite the updates and the heartbeat that thumps
Like a drumroll
And breathing machines and bili lights
The babies always say yes
Despite the screaming ambulances and fire trucks,
Copays, generic or name brand,
Doctor's orders or early morning surgery
The babies always say yes
Despite the shift change, full wards, staff shortages,
On-call physicians stuck in traffic
Or standard procedures
The babies always say yes
Despite sore legs, backs and knees
Despite long shifts, shortened hours, over time
And 1 minute of silence
The babies always say yes
Despite stray bullets, invisible boundaries,
Misguided loyalty, and unwritten rules
The babies always say yes
Despite strained relationships, lost friendships,
Loneliness, adult conversation, and broken families
The babies always say yes
Despite separation, divorce, annulment,

Lawyers, mediators,
Case workers, and child support
The babies always say yes
Despite abuse, abandonment, dependencey, clarity
And relapse
The babies always say yes
Despite legalities, papers, borders,
And government agencies
The babies always say yes
Despite lumps, diagnosis, treatments, counseling,
Remission, and flare-ups
The babies always say yes
And we say
Okay

Broken Glass
dope addict fixing hair and make-up using a piece of a broken mirror

Pretty face in broken glass,
Reflection talking;
> This life won't last,
> Every day goes by so fast.

Living on the third planet from the sun,
So we know,
This life begets yet another one,
Can't stay so close to the fiery ball,
Live – die – live again,
We'll see them all.

Pretty face in broken glass,
Have your fun,
This life won't last,
Every high goes by so fast.

two / sixteen / twenty eleven

I can't get enough,
But you're way too much
Much more than the usual stuff —
So the casual touch is too rough —
Pressure is no better and unwelcome as such —
Clutched arm under arm is a perceivable crutch
So lips talk and toes brush,
Never too much
Never enough

S.I.P.

There's no soundtracks,
Just rabbit fur
Cashmere
And brushed suede —
Muffled pleas
Look the other way
Someone's lucky day falls on your radar.
You're both so far away.

Then the present take its shape —
As the hand molds the clay
And the sun bakes the day.

Rustic Vision — Black Kids

As prosperous as it may seem
Raising entertainers and athletic teams
Some would have us believe
That is the glimmer of hope
So often seen

Passions Of Women

So what for the passions of women,
Confused by what boys like and men demand from them,
Piecing those men together to get a glimpse of the boy
Who's falling apart.
Women,
Shifting their weight side to side-
Family to friends —
Friends to comfort —
Comfort to responsibility —
Responsibility to desire —
Desire to sleep.
What of their passions
Their unknowing battles with one another
Whores and the faithful constantly at odds
And balancing their passion and others on their breasts
What everyone wants —
These pachinko balls that know suffering all too well
Their native tongue is sacrifice, Creole
Or some dialect a man left her with after his use and
Disposal of her,
Women,
The moss on the north side of the tree
The sight at the tip of the barrel
The shoulder that feels the recoil of each blast
They are lava and ash that mysteriously destroy and
Create life with a violent outpour —
We fear the fire,
So we comfort the woman,
And smolder the passion.

Fat Bellies And Fireflies — Sydnee

You're growing
Without me knowing
If I remember you helpless,
Grabbing my hand now only when you need it,
But reaching with both hands,
To remind me of the baby I used to know

Animal Planit

Find your way with me,
Take a chance,
We might look better out of our sheep's clothing,
>Seething,
>Feeding on our prey,
>Partners in crime,
>Predators for a day,
Though the chase beholds the thrill,
The prize was and is still,
The brewing thought ,
Of the next meal

Wake Up Calls

I love your mornings after, get chills
The night before is sweeter still,
Cause by sunrise, there's no surprise

I've closed my eyes many times
Cause by sunrise, it's no surprise

Don't compare my words
To his or hers
Cause by sunrise, there's no surprise

Touch down if you will
I'll fly here still
Cause by sunrise, it's no surprise

You'd be wise to not disguise
Unmask and unveil your lies
Cause by sunrise, there's no surprise.

February 15 —

Give me the mornings after,
No 45 day peaks that drizzle after midnight,
Let the vermin scurry the streets for sweets
That spoil after midnight,
I don't want you to towel off
And lay back down for a little longer,
I want the next day's confusion of what to keep
And what to let go,
Or whose bad habits are more entertaining,
I want your hands tangled with mine,
While we,

        Toast us
        Satisfy senses
        Please palates
        And ease tensions

Lick-O-Wish

Lascivious licorice stick,
Cotton candy hip switch,
Chocolate covered tongue flick,
Powdered sugar lips bit,
Confection conduit,
Slushy slow sip then,
Touch again

Strike A Pose

It's so easy I suppose,
Striking those that are close
Then pose for photos
Promos for what family life should be,
Right,
Hits and kicks be damned,
Faces to the lens,
Photos go as planned,
Family secrets behind smiles and hugs,
Truth,
Be it told,
Scolds and shrugs.

We don't choose the line we are in,
But forgiveness is love,
And love always wins.

Hits and kicks be damned,
Faces to the lens,
Photos go as planned.

Diary Entries

Life is lonely
> You'll cry in cars in empty lots,
> You'll invent reasons to have friends over,
> And beg in silence for them to stay,

Life is lonely
> You'll lie in hospital beds staring at walls and
> Crappy TV programs disgusted with the nurses
> Who woke you up for silly checks,
> But grateful,
> Someone at least took the time to remember you,

Life is lonely
> You'll procrastinate to create an image of
> A busy lifestyle,
> Though everything really only takes a few minutes
> Of your precious time,

Life is lonely
> You need loved ones to tell you, remind you
> How special you are,
> Even though God said it before they knew you

Life is lonely
> And honesty is no remedy,
> It creates space and resentment,
> Hard stares and questions of motive,
> The lie is a tool of unity,
> Even if what we're trying to build is wretched,

Life is lonely
> And there are not enough sunsets to make it better

Apostle Letter

Dear Jesus,

> If you came back as a cricket,
> I'm sorry,
> I wrapped you in toilet paper,
> Threw you in the toilet,
> And peed on you.
>
> In my defense,
> You did say a thief in the night,
> Not a cricket in my bathroom
> In the middle of the day.
>
> Maybe a better warning next time,
> But I'm just saying.

Baby Doll —

Looking at picture of girl who inspired poem "Napalm Song"

I had a baby once
And she was a doll
Softest skin, sweetest smell
No tears to fall

Until the cloud came
And burned us all
      First clothes
      Then skin
      There was nothing left she balled

I saw her and crawled
Wrapped her shell in a shawl
Scrawled her name on a wall
We'll remember the caterwaul

I had a baby once
She was my doll

bRainstorm

lightning in the distance
flickers a warning to the populace at large
of impending danger
the havoc occurs but they will rebuild
the valuables that appreciate with loss
after the rains of course
of course

Good Medicine

Don't you know,
>I would switch positions with you right now,
>Knowing that there's more to you than the pain
>That's handled with machines and pills,

Pain,
That's healed with trust and time
>and follow through
>and remembering
>and talking
>and sitting down
>and slowing down
>and checking in
>and quiet
>and care
>and uncomfortable silence
>and walking away
>and camera's
>and scripts for paid actors

And I have none of these,
But I'd like to think that despite my lackings,
Somehow I've gotten hold of some good medicine

Dagum

Does God know what pain is like,
> The pain that pierces the outer layer of
> Skin,
> And slices and cuts its way through
> The tissue and organs
> Breaking the systems at work,
> Allowing the body to function
> Surviving adverse climates,
> Events,
> Breathing,
> Sending messages of alert
> Calling to arms soldiers that protect us
> From invasion.

Does God know what it's like to feel that nuisance
Of constantly defending fragile territory
Where the possibilities for failure are endless?
Does God understand infinite possibilities
For finite material?
Does God understand visible flaws?
Does God understand work in progress?
Does God understand blind faith?
Does God understand hurt and shortcomings?
Does God understand
Me?

Inns And Outs

It's a quarter passed 2,
    Where are you?
I spent a buck on the room,
    Where are you?
You got an emergency to run to?
    Your mama needs you?
    Me too!
I just called an APB,
Watch out!
For the boys
In blue

Finish Line

Keep up or die,
Vie for a life not less than ordinary,
Crunching numbers for better odds,
A breath from destruction;
It's gotten too far.

A stone's throw from exhaustion,
A card short of a royal flush and heartbreak
Never tasted so greasy going down,
The return trip brings old friends,
This is going to hurt.

Tonight's the night I do believe,
I'll sleep and have that one last dream,
No slow paces, can't go gracefully,
Speed up or die in the doldrums,

I'll draw my own winner's circle,
And drop with gold in my clutches.

I Suppose, I 'Spose

I suppose, I 'spose
To kiss the tip of your nose,

Tho I don't usually do those —
Things

Wiggle it if it itches, wrinkle it even,
But, don't touch it to scratch or rub away sweat and oil,

I'm poised and coiled,
Ready to strike at any moment,

The tip of your nose,
I suppose, I 'spose

The Ritual

The ritual persists
Through headaches, cries, and back rubs
The ritual persists
Through vomit, dry heaves, and diarrhea
The ritual persists
Through questions, prayers, and tears
The ritual persists
Through tests, scans, and needle pricks
The ritual persists
Through discussions, consultations, and conferences
The ritual persists
Through hope, wishes, and probable outcomes
The ritual persists
Through moments, déjà vu, and nightmares
The ritual persists
Through its own doubts and futility
The ritual persists
Through it all without failure, rest or reason

Daddy's Girls

Playgrounds, bikes, and flash cards,
Hide and seek, he'll never find where we are,

Dolls, purses, painted finger and toes,
Story time, music, and puppet shows,

Kisses on scratches, bumps, and face,
Hugs on neck, legs, and waist

August

Periwinkle on your best day
Take the girl and run
You'll find money on the way
Take the limo to the next block
where the street kids stay
Fun for the night
Apologies for tomorrow
Tomorrow okay,

Take the girl and run
You won't be them anyway
You can beat them any day
Leave the limo on the next block
Where the nobody's stay
Money counts but only large amounts
This is where the big boys play,

Take the girl and run
There's baby's on the way
Trade the limo
For gizmos that keep baby's safe,

Take the girl and run
Hold her tighter than you're used to
Since you introduced her to
What the limo was for
But don't let the potholes confuse you

Take the girl and run.

Vermont To Woodson

I bet you'd run up St. Elias
If I could afford the right shoes,
    I got blues baby,
And it's got nothing to do with your overworked lungs,
Or your sisters and their missteps and malfunctions,
    I got blues baby,
And my mother and father didn't miss a birthday,
My sisters took whippings for me,
    I got blues baby,
And your mother's prettier than ever,
She keeps her promises,
    I got blues baby,
And I've had friends,
And late nights I want to remember,
    I got blues baby,
And yellows, and reds, and purples, and greens,
    And you

Kritchuh

Smile for your miracles;
There's marigolds and merry girls.
Say prayers in unison for the debutante,
    Flowers in hand —
    Handsome man at her side —
    Sideways to the camera;
Her photograph's in my memory.
I wanted me in hers
Arm in arm, those were better times,
I'm in on the jokes instead of
Reaching for her other hand
That turns pages in her book.
Reliving a life I can only dream about.

Passion Of Men

What can we say about the passions of men?
Their fathers who cry for the son's misfortune
And hard times,
The slick back haired baby boy who wants
To be cradled by his mother,
The waking giant,
>   Furrowed brow,
>   Wide stance,
>   Uncompromising,
>   Alert,
>   Conducting an army of men charmed by his senses;
Women, yes women
What would man's passion be without the curves
Of a woman?
>   Resting her knee under his hand,
>   Her head in his lap,
>   Her heart accepting his battles ;
His fight for solace and balance,
Learning to answer his own questions,
Is his passion in redeeming himself despite the battle?
>   His heart at the gates of his village,
>   Hung high,
>   Signifying allegiance, honor, valor,
>   It's respect if you ask,
It's the embers of his iris,
It's every flicker of his eye and the tell-tale sign of a war,

       Let passion not smite my progress,
       My notion of power,
       My return into the ocean.
It's taken me once before without warning:
Adrift without sail, engine, or crew,
Abandoned:
Chin in the web of my thumb and index
       Scratching my jaw
       Eyes level with the horizon
       Weighing my options to
Sink or survive.

Waco was born in Galveston, TX on December 12, 1974 and was raised in the Marines. He met his wife in 1996 and has not looked back. She and his daughters have reinvigorated his pen and have been the backbone of his writing. They are the anchor for his wandering mind. Waco uses poetry to get a clear image of what he sees. When he is not writing, Waco likes to swim, bike, run, and ride around the city looking for pancakes. Thoughts on life? In his own words: *youngest of four, only boy, daddy's son, mama's joy.*

The cover photos for this series were contributed by Jon Bidwell, a photographer who lives and works in Kansas. To view more of his work, visit him at www.instagram.com/jonbidwell.

This project was made possible, in part, by generous support from the Osage Arts Community.

Osage Arts Community provides temporary time, space and support for the creation of new artistic works in a retreat format, serving creative people of all kinds — visual artists, composers, poets, fiction and nonfiction writers. Located on a 152-acre farm in an isolated rural mountainside setting in Central Missouri and bordered by ¾ of a mile of the Gasconade River, OAC provides residencies to those working alone, as well as welcoming collaborative teams, offering living space and workspace in a country environment to emerging and mid-career artists. For more information, visit them at osageac.org

Osage Arts Community

www.ingramcontent.com/pod-product-compliance
Lightning Source LLC
Chambersburg PA
CBHW021451080526
44588CB00009B/798